30 fierce dino stickers to decorate your stuff!

DINOSAUR

Bath New York Singapore Hong Kong Cologne Delhi Melbourne

Original text by John Malam
and Steve Parker
Adapted by Jinny Johnson
Consultant: Dr John A. Cooper

This edition published by Parragon in 2009
Parragon
Queen Street House
4 Queen Street
Bath BA1 1HE, UK

ISBN 978-1-4075-7664-0
Printed in China

Contents

The meat-eaters   4

Tyrannosaurus rex   6

Cetiosaurs   8

Diplodocus   10

Stegosaurus   12

Triceratops   14

Iguanodon   16

Plesiosaurs   18

Icthyosaurus   20

Death of the dinosaurs   22

The meat-eaters

All meat-eating dinosaurs are called theropods. The name means 'beast feet'. Most of these dinosaurs moved upright on their slender back legs. They could run fast – much faster than the plant-eaters they hunted.

Creature features

Most of the meat-eating dinosaurs had bird-like feet with clawed toes. They had sharp-clawed hands for attacking and holding onto their prey.

Hand and foot of a meat-eating dinosaur.

Daspletosaurus

Albertosaurus

Dromaeosaurus

Changes over time

Meat-eating dinosaurs adapted over millions of years. Later species were more intelligent and had longer legs and sharper eyes than earlier predators.

Did you know?

A *Tyrannosaurus's* back feet were as much as 1 metre long.

Dromiceiomimus

Troodon

Tyrannosaurus

Dromiceiomimus

Teeth and beaks

Many of the meat-eaters had strong jaws and big teeth. Others had toothless beaks they might have used for cracking eggs.

Tyrannosaurus rex

One of the best known of all dinosaurs, this mighty hunter lived towards the end of the dinosaurs' rule on Earth.

Powerful killer

Tyrannosaurus was strongly built and walked upright on its two big back legs. It held its tail out behind it to help balance the weight of its heavy head and chest. It had good eyesight for spotting its prey at a distance.

Surprise attacker

Tyrannosaurus lived in open woodland and often sneaked up on plant-eating dinosaurs as they stood feeding peacefully. It got as close as it could before making a final high-speed dash and pouncing on its prey.

Big head

Tyrannosaurus had a huge head, up to 1.5 metres long. Its jaws were packed with 50 or 60 razor-sharp teeth. Some were 23 centimetres long.

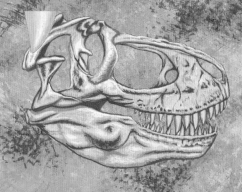

Full to bursting

Like lions and tigers today, *Tyrannosaurus* probably didn't eat every day. If it killed a large plant-eater it would gobble up as much as it could and be satisfied for several days.

Tyrannosaurus bursts out from the trees to attack a group of *Edmontosaurus* dinosaurs.

Small arms

This dinosaur's arms were so tiny they didn't even reach up to its mouth. But its claws were very useful for seizing hold of prey.

Tyrannosaurus facts

Lived: 70 million years ago

Found: North America

Length: 12 metres

Cetiosaurs

These were some of the earliest sauropods. They were all plant-eaters, with a heavy body and a solid backbone. Some later sauropods had bones that were partly hollow, which made them lighter.

Cetiosaurus

Cetiosaurus is famous for being the first sauropod to be discovered. Its giant bones were found in England in 1809.

Barapasaurus

Barapasaurus had a long tail and neck like other cetiosaurs. Its spoon-shaped teeth had jagged edges for stripping leaves from branches.

Barapasaurus facts

Lived: 200 million years ago

Found: Asia

Length: 18 metres

Cetiosaurus facts

Lived: 175 million years ago

Found: Europe, Africa

Length: 18 metres

Shunosaurus facts

Lived: 170 million years ago

Found: China

Length: 10 metres

Shunosaurus

This cetiosaur had a spiky lump of bone at the end of its tail. It could use this to defend itself against attackers.

Diplodocus

This is one of the biggest and best known of the diplodocids. Experts used to think it dragged its tail on the ground. But fossilized tracks show that it held its tail up as it walked.

Fern-eater

Diplodocus probably couldn't lift its head very high. So it may have eaten mainly low-growing plants such as ferns.

10-tonne beast

Although *Diplodocus* was so long, it weighed only 10 tonnes. This was less than some other sauropods. The dinosaur was light for its size because many of the bones in its spine were hollow.

Extra bones

There was an extra bone beneath each of the vertebrae making up *Diplodocus*'s backbone. These strengthened its tail.

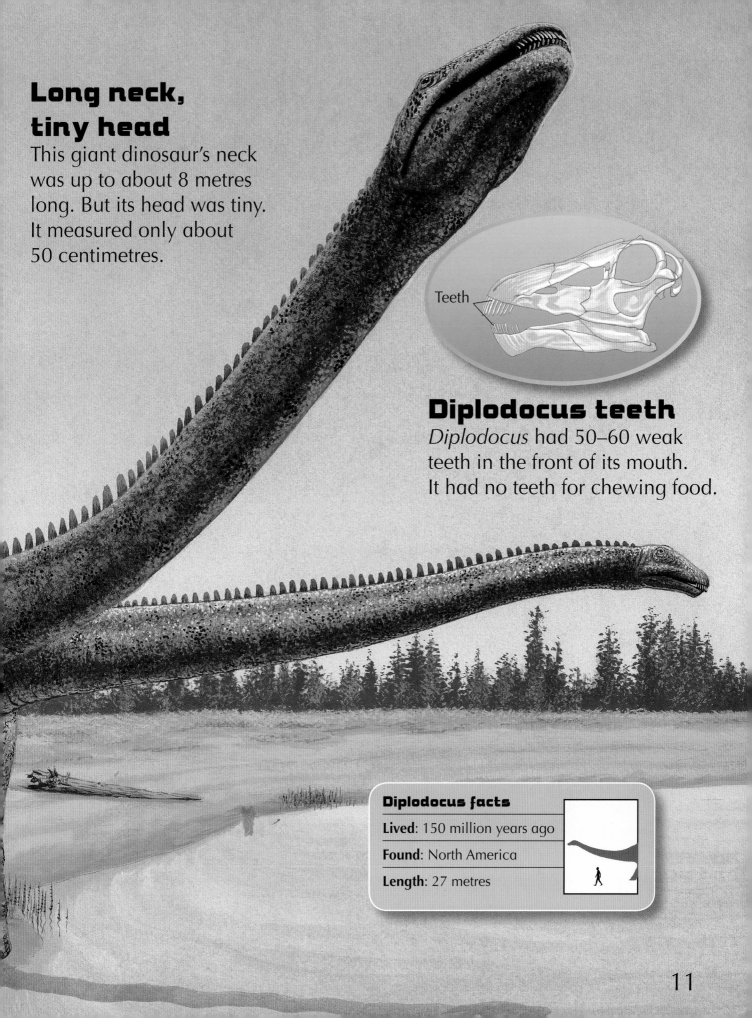

Long neck, tiny head

This giant dinosaur's neck was up to about 8 metres long. But its head was tiny. It measured only about 50 centimetres.

Teeth

Diplodocus teeth

Diplodocus had 50–60 weak teeth in the front of its mouth. It had no teeth for chewing food.

Diplodocus facts

Lived: 150 million years ago

Found: North America

Length: 27 metres

Stegosaurus

Stegosaurus was the biggest stegosaur. Lots of fossils have been found so it is also the best known of its family.

Roof reptile

When fossils of this dinosaur were first found, experts thought that the bony plates lay flat, covering the animal's back like a turtle's shell. Because of this, the dinosaur was given the name *Stegosaurus*, which means 'roofed reptile'. Later they realized that the plates actually stood upright.

The tail

Stegosaurus was a slow-moving plant-eater. It probably moved around in small groups. If attacked, *Stegosaurus* could not run away very fast so it stood still and hit out against its enemy with its spiky tail.

Stegosaurus plate pattern

Experts aren't sure how the bony plates were arranged. They may have been in one row, in pairs or overlapping in a staggered row.

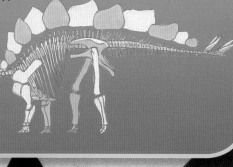

Two males fight over a female *Stegosaurus*. They turn their bodies sideways to show off their full size.

Stegosaurus facts

Lived: 140 million years ago

Found: North America

Length: 9 metres

Triceratops

Triceratops is the most famous of the ceratopsians, or horned dinosaurs. It had three sharp horns on its head, and its name means 'three-horned face'.

Strong body

Triceratops had a big chunky body, short tail and thick legs. It weighed about 10 tonnes and was strong enough to fight off even fierce hunters such as tyrannosaurs.

Triceratops skull

This dinosaur's neck frill was made of solid bone. The horns on top of its head were up to 1m long, but the nose horn was smaller.

Frill

Horn

Hole for eye

Nose horn

Nostril

Some adult *Triceratops* fight off a tyrannosaur.

Triceratops facts

Lived: 70 million years ago

Found: North America

Length: 9 metres

Protecting the weak

Triceratops lived in a group, or herd, of animals. Young animals stayed in the centre of the group where they were safer from attackers.

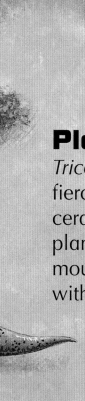

Plant-eater

Triceratops looks very fierce, but like other ceratopsians it ate only plants. It bit off mouthfuls of leaves with its sharp beak.

Big battles

Triceratops probably fought over mates or who would lead the herd. They crashed their heads together and locked horns.

15

Iguanodon

This was only the second dinosaur ever to be named. It was called *Iguanodon*, which means 'iguana teeth', because its teeth looked like those of the iguana lizard.

Horse head

Iguanodon was a big animal with a long, stiff tail. It had a long head like a horse and its jaws were filled with lots of sharp teeth.

Two legs or four

This dinosaur could walk upright on its two back legs or on all fours. It could run at speeds of up to 20 kilometres per hour.

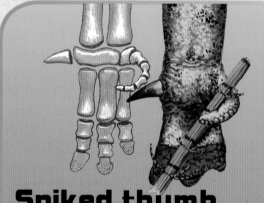

Spiked thumb

Iguanodon had four clawed fingers and a big spiky thumb. It could bend its little finger across its hand to help it hold onto things, such as twigs and leaves.

Ground to a pulp

Using the strong beak at the front of its mouth, *Iguanodon* bit off leaves and twigs to eat. It chewed its food for a long time until it was just a mushy pulp.

Using the thumb

Iguanodon could have used its thumb spike like a dagger to defend itself from meat-eating dinosaurs.

Iguanodon facts

Lived: 130 million years ago

Found: Asia, Europe, N. America

Length: 10 metres

Plesiosaurs

These sea-living reptiles first lived about 200 million years ago. They had small heads and long necks. They fed mostly on fish and other small sea creatures.

Plesiosaurus

This was one of the first plesiosaurs. Like other plesiosaurs, it probably 'flew' through the water by flapping its long flippers up and down, like turtles do today.

Plesiosaurus facts

Lived: 200 million years ago

Found: Europe

Length: 2.5 metres

Cryptoclidus facts

Lived: 150 million years ago

Found: Europe

Length: 4 metres

Cryptoclidus

Cryptoclidus had many smaller joints in its flippers. This gave the flipper a smoother and more flexible curved surface.

Caught in a cage

A plesiosaur's toothy jaws made a trap for prey. When the reptile opened its mouth, water and fish flowed in. When it closed its mouth, the fish were trapped inside.

Long curved flippers for swimming power

Muraenosaurus

Half the length of this huge creature was its neck, and its head was very tiny. It probably swung its neck to and fro as it snapped up mouthfuls of food.

Muraenosaurus facts	
Lived: 150 million years ago	
Found: Europe	
Length: 6 metres	

Ichthyosaurus

Lots of fossils of this reptile have been found, so it is one of the best known of all prehistoric animals. This species lived for more than 60 million years.

Fossil food

Ichthyosaurus ate fish, squid and curly-shelled ammonites. Fossils of all these creatures have been found with ichthyosaur remains.

Big eyes for hunting

Skeletons show that ichthyosaurs had very big eyes. A species called *Ophthalmosaurus* had the largest. They were 10 centimetres across.

Super senses

Ichthyosaurus's big eyes helped it see in the darkness of the deep ocean. It could also sense ripples in the water, made by moving prey, with its ears.

Fine fossils

Some of the ichthyosaur fossils that have been found are in very good condition. They have many bones arranged next to each other as they would have been when the animal was alive.

Ichthyosaurus could crack an ammonite's hard shell with its strong jaws.

How deep?

We don't know how deep *Ichthyosaurus* could dive to find prey. Relatives of the type of squid it ate live in very deep sea today, down to 1000 metres.

Eggs or babies?

Ichthyosaurus could not come to land to lay eggs. It gave birth to its young in the water, like dolphins do today.

Ichthyosaurus facts

Lived: 200 million years ago

Found: Europe, N. America

Length: 1.8 metres

Death of the dinosaurs

From time to time lots of living things die out. About 65 million years ago, dinosaurs and many other creatures disappeared.

Not only dinosaurs

Flying reptiles called pterosaurs in the air, and mosasaurs and plesiosaurs in the sea also became extinct around 65 million years ago.

How long?

Dinosaurs were wiped out 65 million years ago. But this did not happen instantly. By 70 million years ago there were already fewer dinosaurs than before.

The asteroid impact

An asteroid is a piece of rock from space. Some people think that an asteroid hit the Earth 65 million years ago.

1. Asteroid hits the Earth

2. Impact of the explosion spreads quickly

3. Dust and debris cause climate change

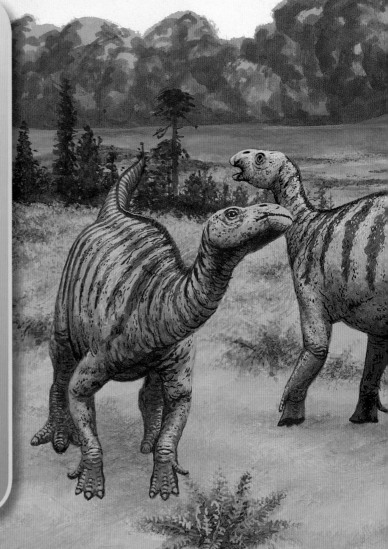

The asteroid idea

If an asteroid did hit the Earth 65 million years ago it would have caused huge clouds of dust and debris to spread. This would have blocked out the sun for years, so plants died. Without plants, plant-eating animals died, too, and then meat-eating animals.

An enormous crater found off the coast of Mexico may have been the asteroid's impact site.

Did you know?

The asteroid of 65 million years ago might have measured 10 kilometres across and travelled at 55 kilometres per second.

Acknowledgements

Cover: Front – Joe Drivas/GettyImages, back – Anatole Branch/GettyImages, StockTrek/GettyImages.

Poster and page 24: Jon Hughes and Russell Gooday, http://www.pixel-shack.com.

Internal illustrations by:
Norma Burgin, Mark Dolby, Graham Kennedy, Peter Komarnysky, Damian Quayle,
Neil Reed, Pete Roberts (Allied Artists), James Field, Terry Riley (SGA), Mike Atkinson,
Chris Forsey, Rob Shone, Q2A Media.